KETOGENIC GREEN SMOOTHIES

Ketogenic Recipes To Detox And Cleanse To
Boost Health And Healing

Melissa Petitto, RD

chartwell
books

Introduction 4

Beverages

Antioxidant Smoothie 8
Detox Smoothie 10
The Power Player Smoothie 12
Cleanse Me Smoothie 14
Glowing Skin Smoothie 16
Blue-Green Algae Smoothie 18

Chia, Kale, and Pineapple Smoothie 20
Creamy Fennel and Pear Smoothie 22
Celery and Pear Smoothie 24
Celery, Apple, and Almond Butter Smoothie 26
Anti-inflammatory Smoothie 28
Maca and Coconut Smoothie 30
Blueberry and Coconut Smoothie 32

Immunity Smoothie 34
Celery, Tomato, Basil, and Avocado Smoothie 36
Broccoli-Banana Smoothie 38
Metabolism-Boosting Smoothie 40
Simple Blender Celery Juice 42
Super Prebiotic Baobab Juice 44

Digestion Juice 46
Celery, Apple, and Lemon Juice 48
Kidney Detox Juice 50
Cellulite Buster 52
Liver Detox Juice 54
Arthritis Helper 56

Snacks, Soups, and Salads

Creamy Celery Soup 60
Spicy Thai Salad 62
Fennel and Celery Slaw with Walnuts 64
Crunchy Pomegranate Guacamole 66
Double Celery Salad with Spicy Horseradish Dressing 68
Sicilian Celery, Asian Pear, Fennel, and Orange Slaw with Toasted Hazelnuts 70

Simply Divine Celery Broth 72
Baobab Gazpacho 74
Spicy Purple Potato Salad 76
Celery Juice Pulp Fritters 78
Green Juice Pulp Crackers 80
Pulp-sicles 82
Celery Pulp Hummus 84

Juice Pulp Veggie Burgers 86
Juice Pulp "Meat" Balls 88
Juice Pulp Granola 90
Pistachio Green Juice Pulp Pesto 92
Veggie-Packed Vegetable Broth 94

Introduction

While hype for green juice abounds, the visible health benefits speak for themselves. Hydrating and full of valuable vitamins and minerals and a variety of other nutrients your body craves, green veggies should be a staple in everyone's diet. Juicing and blending them in your day-to-day life can lead to weight loss, balanced blood sugar levels, reduced inflammation, additional energy, and help strengthen your body against a variety of chronic illnesses. This is especially true if you're following a ketogenic diet.

Ketogenic Green Smoothies provides a variety of yummy ways to ease yourself into this healthy habit. Your crash course includes more than 20 green juice and smoothie recipes, how to make veggie juices from a blender, and ideas beyond just juice and smoothies.

The shelf life of a juice is very short; optimally, you should drink it within 30 minutes of preparing it, but if you must store it, store it in the refrigerator for no longer than 48 hours. And what do you do with all the leftover pulp? Don't throw it away! See the Snacks, Soups, and Salads section for ways to use it in everything from fritters to crackers to soups.

JUICES VS. SMOOTHIES

I am frequently asked about the differences between juicing and smoothies. Both contain fruits and vegetables, which contain high amounts of vitamins, minerals, enzymes, and other incredible phytonutrients. Phytonutrients are plant- derived compounds associated with disease prevention and are beneficial for those seeking to live a healthier lifestyle. While both are essentially a beverage, there are separate benefits for consuming your favorite plant-based smoothies or juices.

Juicing is the process where you separate the liquid from the pulp or fiber of the fruit or vegetable. The product you get is a thin and concentrated liquid that contains all of the nutrients listed above. The removal of dietary fiber is an advantage to juicing. The body doesn't need to work as hard to extract all of these amazing vitamins, minerals, enzymes, and phytonutrients from the plants you have juiced. This allows the nutrients to enter your bloodstream as quickly as possible and with the least amount of energy expended by the body. (No juicer? No problem. See page 42 for blender directions.)

Smoothies come from blending the entire fruit, vegetable, liquid, nuts, seeds, and other various superfoods, which adds the necessary fat and protein if you're following a keto diet. The result frequently has more volume, thickness, and is generally creamier than a juice. With smoothies, you retain the fiber, which makes you feel full and improves digestion.

I often think of a smoothie as a meal replacer and a juice as a beverage. With smoothies, you are getting all of the same amazing nutrients as you would from a juice, but with the addition of soluble and dietary fiber. Your body may have to work harder to extract the nutrients and fiber from a smoothie, but sometimes it helps to feel full.

BEVERAGES

Antioxidant Smoothie

Yield: 2 servings

I know, I know: collard greens in a smoothie?! But why not? These dark leafy greens are a part of the cruciferous family and are high in nutrients and antioxidants that fight cell-damaging free radicals. This smoothie is a perfect start to the day.

INGREDIENTS

1 cup (40 g) organic collard greens, thick stems removed
2 organic celery stalks
1 organic Fuji apple
½ cup (85 g) organic frozen pineapple chunks
½ cup (120 ml) unsweetened almond or hemp milk

METHOD OF PREPARATION:

1. Wash and roughly chop all the vegetables. Core and quarter the apple.
2. Place all the ingredients into a high-powered blender and blend on high speed until smooth and creamy.
3. Serve immediately for optimal vitamin and mineral content.

Detox Smoothie

Yield: 2 servings

This green smoothie is optimal for great digestion. With anti-inflammatory and nutrient-rich kiwi and celery, this naturally detoxifying juice is a perfect way to cleanse the body.

INGREDIENTS

6 organic celery stalks
2 organic kiwis, peeled
1 cup (30 g) organic baby spinach
2 organic parsley sprigs
1 organic lime, juiced
1 organic lemon, juiced
½ cup (120 ml) freshly squeezed orange juice

METHOD OF PREPARATION:

1. Wash and roughly chop all the vegetables.
2. Place all the ingredients into a high-powered blender and blend on high speed until smooth and creamy.
3. Serve immediately for optimal vitamin and mineral content.

The Power Player Smoothie

Yield: 2 servings

This smoothie is bursting with antioxidants, vitamins, and minerals. It's not for the faint of heart, though! Beets, ginger, and celery come together for quite a powerful punch that will leave you feeling awake and rejuvenated.

INGREDIENTS

2 organic celery stalks
2 organic small red beets, washed and trimmed
1 organic Fuji apple
½ cup (85 g) organic frozen peaches
1½ cups (360 ml) unsweetened almond or hemp milk
1-inch (2.5 cm) piece organic ginger, peeled

METHOD OF PREPARATION:

1. Wash and roughly chop all the vegetaebles. Core and quarter the apple.
2. Place all the ingredients into a high-powered blender and blend on high speed until smooth and creamy.
3. Serve immediately for optimal vitamin and mineral content.

Cleanse Me Smoothie

Yield: 2 servings

This super gentle and cleansing smoothie is perfect for when your body just needs a little break and reboot. It is clean, low-calorie, and wonderfully filling.

INGREDIENTS

1 cup (30 g) organic baby spinach
2 organic celery stalks
½ avocado, peeled
2 organic parsley sprigs
½ cup (120 g) ice cubes
1½ cups (360 ml) coconut water
1 tablespoon (15 ml) freshly squeezed lemon juice

METHOD OF PREPARATION:

1. Wash and roughly chop all the vegetables.
2. Place all the ingredients into a high-powered blender and blend on high speed until smooth and creamy.
3. Serve immediately for optimal vitamin and mineral content.

Glowing Skin Smoothie

Yield: 2 servings

This smoothie is packed with antioxidants that aid in giving skin that beautiful glow from the inside out. Avocado, spinach, celery, blueberries, and carrots come together to deliver one glowing boost.

INGREDIENTS

1 cup (30 g) organic baby spinach
2 organic celery stalks
1 medium organic carrot, peeled
½ avocado, peeled
1 organic pear
1 cup (145 g) frozen organic blueberries
1½ cups (360 ml) unsweetened almond or hemp milk

METHOD OF PREPARATION:

1. Wash and roughly chop all the vegetables. Core and quarter the pear.
2. Place all the ingredients into a high-powered blender and blend on high speed until smooth and creamy.
3. Serve immediately for optimal vitamin and mineral content.

Blue-Green Algae Smoothie

Yield: 2 servings

I know the title may throw you, but algae is a superfood! It's high in antioxidants, has inflammation-fighting properties, and helps regulate the immune system. Don't shy away because of the name; the color alone could change your mind.

INGREDIENTS

4 organic celery stalks
1 cup (150 g) organic frozen green grapes
1 large organic cucumber
1 frozen peeled banana, chopped
½ avocado, peeled
1 cup (30 g) organic baby spinach
2 organic cilantro sprigs
1 tablespoon (8 g) blue spirulina powder
1-inch (2.5 cm) piece organic ginger, peeled
1 cup (240 ml) coconut water

METHOD OF PREPARATION:

1. Wash and roughly chop all the vegetables.
2. Place all the ingredients into a high-powered blender and blend on high speed until smooth and creamy.
3. Serve immediately for optimal vitamin and mineral content.

Chia, Kale, and Pineapple Smoothie

Yield: 2 servings

This delicious smoothie has a tropical hint with creamy coconut milk and pineapple. The chia seeds give this smoothie a thicker texture and a big hit of omega-3s.

INGREDIENTS

4 organic celery stalks
2 cups (120 g) chopped organic kale, large stems removed
1½ cups (248 g) organic frozen pineapple chunks
2 tablespoons (22 g) chia seeds
1½ cups (360 ml) unsweetened coconut milk

METHOD OF PREPARATION:

1. Wash and roughly chop all the vegetables.
2. Place all the ingredients into a high-powered blender and blend on high speed until smooth and creamy.
3. Serve immediately for optimal vitamin and mineral content.

Creamy Fennel and Pear Smoothie

Yield: 2 servings

Fennel and celery are natural digestion aids. Combined with the alkalizing effects of the lemon juice, this smoothie is a wonderful way to calm the stomach and support good digestion.

INGREDIENTS

1 organic fennel bulb, cored
2 organic celery stalks
2 organic ripe pears
4 ounces (112 g) almond or coconut yogurt
⅓ cup (80 ml) freshly squeezed lemon juice
1 teaspoon fennel seeds

METHOD OF PREPARATION:

1. Wash and roughly chop all the vegetables. Core and quarter the pears.
2. Place all the ingredients into a high-powered blender and blend on high speed until smooth and creamy.
3. Serve immediately for optimal vitamin and mineral content.

Celery and Pear Smoothie

Yield: 2 servings

Creamy, earthy, and chock-full of fiber, this smoothie hits all the points.

INGREDIENTS

3 organic celery stalks
1 cup (30 g) organic baby spinach
1 organic ripe pear
1 avocado, peeled and pitted
2 tablespoons (30 ml) freshly squeezed lemon juice
1 cup (240 ml) coconut water

METHOD OF PREPARATION:

1. Wash and roughly chop all vegetables. Core and quarter the pear.
2. Place all the ingredients into a high-powered blender and blend on high speed until smooth and creamy.
3. Serve immediately for optimal vitamin and mineral content.

Celery, Apple, and Almond Butter Smoothie

Yield: 2 servings

This smoothie hits all the breakfast points: servings of vegetables and fruit, hydration, and protein. This quick and easy smoothie is a perfect start to the day.

INGREDIENTS

4 organic celery stalks
2 cups (60 g) organic baby spinach
2 organic Fuji apples
¼ cup (60 g) organic almond butter
1½ cups (360 ml) coconut water

METHOD OF PREPARATION:

1. Wash and roughly chop all the vegetables. Core and quarter the apples.
2. Place all the ingredients into a high-powered blender and blend on high speed until smooth and creamy.
3. Serve immediately for optimal vitamin and mineral content.

Anti-Inflammatory Smoothie

Yield: 2 servings

This powerful anti-inflammatory smoothie is packed with vitamins and nutrients. Cinnamon, ginger, and turmeric all help reduce inflammation in the body, decrease pain, and give you an immune boost. This smoothie is a warming one for the cold winter months.

INGREDIENTS

2 organic celery stalks
1 medium organic carrot
1 small organic cucumber
1 organic Fuji apple
1 tablespoon organic almond butter
¼ teaspoon organic turmeric powder
1-inch (2.5 cm) piece organic ginger, peeled
1 teaspoon ground cinnamon
¼ cup (60 ml) unsweetened coconut milk
1 cup (240 ml) coconut water
1 cup (240 g) ice cubes

METHOD OF PREPARATION:

1. Wash and roughly chop all the vegetables. Core and quarter the apple.
2. Place all the ingredients into a high-powered blender and blend on high speed until smooth and creamy.
3. Serve immediately for optimal vitamin and mineral content.

Maca and Coconut Smoothie

Yield: 2 servings

Maca powder is known for improving sexual function in both men and women, and it is an energy booster. If too much is taken, it can exasperate hormonal issues, though, so always stick to the recommended dosage. Maca is a great source of protein, as well as vitamins B1, B2, B12, C and E. The combination of maca, celery, and coconut is slightly sweet and refreshing.

INGREDIENTS

8 organic celery stalks
2 organic Fuji apples
2 frozen peeled bananas, chopped
1 teaspoon maca powder
1 teaspoon coconut oil
1 tablespoon (6 g) unsweetened coconut flakes
1 teaspoon chlorella powder

METHOD OF PREPARATION:

1. Wash and roughly chop the celery. Core and quarter the apples.
2. Place all the ingredients into a high-powered blender and blend on high speed until smooth and creamy.
3. Serve immediately for optimal vitamin and mineral content.

Blueberry and Coconut Smoothie

Yield: 2 servings

This smoothie is rich in vitamin C, potassium, and fiber. With its sweet, creamy texture and cholesterol-lowering benefits, this smoothie will become one of your all-time favorites for a quick and easy snack.

INGREDIENTS

6 organic celery stalks
1 frozen peeled banana, chopped
2 cups (290 g) organic frozen blueberries
2 cups (480 ml) coconut water
1 tablespoon (6 g) unsweetened coconut flakes

METHOD OF PREPARATION:

1. Wash and roughly chop the celery.
2. Place all the ingredients into a high-powered blender and blend on high speed until smooth and creamy.
3. Serve immediately for optimal vitamin and mineral content.

Immunity Smoothie

Yield: 2 servings

This smoothie is a natural body coolant and immune booster. It's packed with fiber, iron, beta-carotene, and vitamins A, C, and E.

INGREDIENTS

2 organic celery stalks
2 organic carrots, peeled
1 cup (174 g) pomegranate arils
1 cup (240 ml) unsweetened almond or hemp milk

METHOD OF PREPARATION:

1. Wash and roughly chop the vegetables.
2. Place all the ingredients into a high-powered blender and blend on high speed until smooth and creamy.
3. Serve immediately for optimal vitamin and mineral content.

Celery, Tomato, Basil, and Avocado Smoothie

Yield: 2 servings

Don't know what to do with all of those summer tomatoes? Make a smoothie! This delightful and filling smoothie combines some of my favorite ingredients for a vitamin–and healthy fat-packed drinkable lunch.

INGREDIENTS

2 organic celery stalks
3 large organic heirloom tomatoes
1 large avocado, peeled and pitted
2 organic basil sprigs
1 cup (240 ml) water
1 organic lime, peeled

METHOD OF PREPARATION:

1. Wash and roughly chop all the vegetables.
2. Place all the ingredients into a high-powered blender and blend on high speed until smooth and creamy.
3. Serve immediately for optimal vitamin and mineral content.

Broccoli-Banana Smoothie

Yield: 2 servings

This smoothie sounds strange, I know, but pulverizing your broccoli in a smoothie and masking its flavor is a great way to get twice the daily amount of vitamin C and half the daily amount of vitamin A.

INGREDIENTS

2 organic celery stalks
2 cups (142 g) organic broccoli florets
2 organic Fuji apples
1 frozen peeled banana, chopped
1 tablespoon (20 g) raw local honey
1½ cups (360 ml) unsweetened almond or hemp milk

METHOD OF PREPARATION:

1. Wash and roughly chop the vegetables. Core and quarter the apples.
2. Place all the ingredients into a high-powered blender and blend on high speed until smooth and creamy.
3. Serve immediately for optimal vitamin and mineral content.

Metabolism-Boosting Smoothie

Yield: 2 servings

The combination of spinach, mint, celery, green tea, grapefruit, pineapple, avocado, and cayenne is a complex one! This smoothie, with its healthy fats, protein, complex carbohydrates, vitamins, and minerals is a perfect start to the day to boost your metabolism.

INGREDIENTS

2 cups (60 g) organic baby spinach
2 organic celery stalks
1 large organic pink grapefruit, peeled
2 cups (330 g) frozen organic pineapple chunks
1 large avocado, peeled and pitted
1 cup (240 ml) brewed green tea, cooled
2 organic mint sprigs
Pinch of cayenne pepper

METHOD OF PREPARATION:

1. Wash and roughly chop the vegetables and fruit.
2. Place all the ingredients into a high-powered blender and blend on high speed until smooth and creamy.
3. Serve immediately for optimal vitamin and mineral content.

Simple Blender Celery Juice

Yield: 1 serving

The amount of celery needed will differ. You are aiming for 16 ounces (480 ml) of celery juice for optimal results. This can be made in a juicer, but I want to show that you can make it without the investment in a large appliance. Buy yourself a couple of nut milk bags for ease, but if you can't find those, a fine-mesh strainer will do the trick! Drink immediately, first thing in the morning, on an empty stomach. This method can be used with any and all of the juices if buying a juicer is not in the budget.

INGREDIENTS

1 large bunch organic celery
1 nut milk bag

METHOD OF PREPARATION:

1. Cut the bottom root off of the celery and rinse each individual stalk.
2. Chop the celery and, working in batches, add to a high-powered blender and blend on high speed until smooth and all the celery has been added.
3. Fit your nut milk bag over a glass measuring cup. Pour the celery puree into the nut milk bag and squeeze until all the liquid is removed and you have 16 ounces (480 ml).
4. Reserve the pulp for another use and drink the juice immediately for optimal vitamin and nutrient content.

Super Prebiotic Baobab Juice

Yield: 4 servings

Baobab is one of my favorite superfoods and it is an excellent prebiotic. I am a fan of the Kaibae brand; not only is it superiorly made, but it also gives back to Ghanian people and their cherished baobab tree. Baobab is an antioxidant powerhouse, making this juice a go-to for wellness.

INGREDIENTS

4 organic celery stalks

1 small head organic green cabbage, outer leaves removed and cut into small chunks

1 organic fennel bulb, cored and cut into quarters

2 organic green apples, cored and quartered

4 teaspoons baobab powder

METHOD OF PREPARATION:

1. Pass the celery, cabbage, fennel, and apples through your juicer. Reserve the pulp for another use. (See page 42 for blender directions.)
2. Divide the mixture among four glasses and stir in 1 teaspoon of baobab powder per glass. Serve immediately for optimal vitamin and nutrient content.

Digestion Juice

Yield: 2 servings

This combination of celery, cucumber, orange, and lemon is super refreshing and has the added benefit of supporting good digestion.

INGREDIENTS

1 large bunch organic celery
2 large organic cucumbers
1 organic navel orange, peeled
½ organic lemon, peeled

METHOD OF PREPARATION:

1. Wash all the ingredients and roughly chop.
2. Pass all the ingredients through your juicer. (See page 42 for blender directions.) Serve immediately for optimal vitamin and nutrient content.

Celery, Apple, and Lemon Juice

Yield: 2 servings

This is a super refreshing and delicious combination, as well as a simple detox for the body. If you do not have a juicer, follow the simple celery juice recipe (page 42) that is made in a blender.

INGREDIENTS

4 organic celery stalks
1 organic Fuji apple
2 cups (60 g) organic baby spinach
½ organic lemon

METHOD OF PREPARATION:

1. Wash and chop the celery, and core and chop the apple.
2. Pass the celery, apple, and spinach through your juicer. Reserve the pulp for another use.
3. To serve, squeeze the lemon juice into the mixture and serve immediately for optimal vitamin and nutrient content.

Kidney Detox Juice

Yield: 2 servings

This simple three-ingredient juice, made with celery, parsley, and pineapple, is a sure-fire way to detox the kidneys, as well as a natural diuretic and circulatory catalyst.

INGREDIENTS

6 organic celery stalks
1 bunch organic parsley
2 cups (330 g) organic pineapple chunks

METHOD OF PREPARATION:

1. Wash the celery and parsley and roughly chop.
2. Pass all the ingredients through your juicer. Reserve the pulp for another use. (See page 42 for blender directions.)
3. Serve immediately for optimal vitamin and nutrient content.

Cellulite Buster

Yield: 2 servings

The combination of celery, apple, pear, pink grapefruit, and mint is not only a delicious one but also has been shown to improve circulation, enhance collagen production, improve skin elasticity, and reduce fluid retention. What a juice!

INGREDIENTS

4 organic celery stalks
2 organic Fuji apples
1 organic pear
1 large organic pink grapefruit, peeled
4 organic mint sprigs

METHOD OF PREPARATION:

1. Wash all the ingredients and chop the celery. Core and chop the apples and pear. Chop the grapefruit into segments.
2. Pass all the ingredients through your juicer. Reserve the pulp for another use. (See page 42 for blender directions.)
3. Serve immediately for optimal vitamin and mineral content.

Liver Detox Juice

Yield: 2 servings

Celery, cucumber, asparagus, parsley, cilantro, and lemon make this powerful juice a natural diuretic and hydrator. The liver aids in immunity, digestion, nutrient absorption, and skin vitality. This juice helps keep that liver super happy.

INGREDIENTS

5 organic celery stalks
1 large organic cucumber
3 organic asparagus spears
2 organic parsley sprigs
2 organic cilantro sprigs
1 organic lemon, peeled

METHOD OF PREPARATION:

1. Wash all the ingredients and cut into chunks.
2. Pass all the ingredients through your juicer. Reserve the pulp for another use. (See page 42 for blender directions.)
3. Serve immediately for optimal vitamin and mineral content.

Arthritis Helper

Yield: 2 servings

Pineapple is a natural anti-inflammatory food. It contains bromelain, which works as a natural anti-inflammatory substance for swollen and painful joints.

INGREDIENTS

6 large organic carrots
3 organic celery stalks
1 cup (165 g) organic pineapple chunks
½ organic lemon, peeled

METHOD OF PREPARATION:

1. Wash all the ingredients and roughly chop.
2. Pass all the ingredients through your juicer. Reserve the pulp for another use. (See page 42 for blender directions.)
3. Serve immediately for optimal vitamin and mineral content.

SNACKS, SOUPS, AND SALADS

Creamy Celery Soup

Yield: 4 servings

This decadent, creamy celery soup is dairy-free and oh so delicious. I love this soup straight out of a mug on a cold and dreary day for the perfect comfort food.

INGREDIENTS

¼ cup (60 ml) olive oil
1 sweet onion, diced
2 leeks, cleaned, white and light green parts thinly sliced
1 large bunch organic celery, chopped
6 garlic cloves, minced
1 tablespoon (2.5 g) organic chopped fresh thyme
6 cups (1440 ml) vegetable stock
2 teaspoons sea salt
1 teaspoon freshly ground black pepper
½ cup (120 ml) unsweetened almond half-and-half

METHOD OF PREPARATION:

1. Heat the oil in a large Dutch oven over medium heat. Add the onion, leeks, and celery and sauté for 10 minutes. Add the garlic and thyme and sauté for another minute or until fragrant.
2. Add the stock, salt, and pepper. Increase the heat to high and bring the soup to a boil, then reduce the heat to low, cover the Dutch oven, and simmer for 20 minutes.
3. Remove the soup from the heat and add the half-and-half. Use an immersion blender to blend the soup until thick and creamy.
4. Serve hot.

Spicy Thai Salad

Yield: 4 servings

The crunch of celery with the spiciness of the chiles and saltiness of the peanuts is going to make this one of your favorite go-to simple salads.

INGREDIENTS

3 tablespoons (45 ml) toasted sesame oil
3 tablespoons (45 ml) freshly squeezed lime juice
2 teaspoons fish sauce or tamari
8 organic celery stalks, thinly sliced
3 scallions, thinly sliced
1 Fresno chile, thinly sliced
½ cup (8 g) organic cilantro leaves
½ cup (20 g) organic Thai basil leaves
¼ cup (5 g) organic mint leaves
¼ cup (10 g) organic celery leaves
¼ cup (35 g) roasted, salted peanuts, chopped

METHOD OF PREPARATION:

1. In a small bowl, whisk together the sesame oil, lime juice, and fish sauce or tamari.
2. In a large bowl, combine the celery, scallions, chile, cilantro, basil, mint, and celery leaves. Add the dressing and toss to combine.
3. Sprinkle with the peanuts and serve immediately.

Fennel and Celery Slaw with Walnuts

Yield: 4 servings

I love a simple coleslaw, and the crunch of this one is unparalleled. The walnuts on top give it an extra crunchy boost. Try this on top of your favorite grilled fish or as a simple BBQ side dish.

INGREDIENTS

1 shallot, minced
2 tablespoons (22 g) whole-grain mustard
1 teaspoon raw local honey
½ cup (120 ml) sherry vinegar
⅓ cup (80 ml) extra virgin olive oil
1 teaspoon sea salt
2 organic fennel bulbs, cored and thinly shaved
10 organic celery stalks, thinly sliced on the diagonal
1 cup (145 g) shelled whole walnuts, toasted and chopped

METHOD OF PREPARATION:

1. To make the coleslaw, in a large bowl, whisk together the minced shallot, mustard, honey, vinegar, olive oil, and salt.
2. Add the shaved fennel and shaved celery to the dressing. Toss to coat.
3. To serve, arrange the slaw on a platter and sprinkle with the chopped glazed walnuts.

Crunchy Pomegranate Guacamole

Yield: 4 servings

Who doesn't love guacamole? This one is taken to a whole new level with the crunch and pop of celery and pomegranate arils.

INGREDIENTS

½ small red onion, diced
½ cup (87 g) pomegranate arils
½ cup (75 g) grape tomatoes, chopped
½ jalapeño, diced (seeded for less heat)
1 organic celery stalk, diced
¼ cup (4 g) organic cilantro, washed and chopped
Juice of 2 limes
1 teaspoon sea salt
3 large ripe avocados, peeled and pitted
Tortilla chips, for serving

METHOD OF PREPARATION:

1. In a large bowl, combine the diced onion, pomegranate arils, grape tomatoes, jalapeño, celery, cilantro, lime juice, and sea salt.
2. Add the avocados and mash to combine. Check the seasoning and serve with tortilla chips.

Double Celery Salad with Spicy Horseradish Dressing

Yield: 4 servings

This salad is a great addition to a heavy main dish. It's light and fresh and crunchy and a tad spicy.

INGREDIENTS

1 medium shallot, diced
2 tablespoons (30 g) prepared horseradish
¼ cup (60 ml) freshly squeezed lemon juice
½ cup (120 ml) extra virgin olive oil
½ teaspoon sea salt
½ teaspoon freshly ground black pepper
1 medium organic celery root, peeled and julienned on a mandoline
1 bunch organic celery, thinly sliced on the diagonal
½ cup (20 g) organic celery leaves
½ cup (20 g) organic parsley leaves
Sprinkling of capers (optional)

METHOD OF PREPARATION:

1. In a large bowl, whisk together the shallot, horseradish, lemon juice, olive oil, salt, and pepper.
2. Add the celery root, celery, celery leaves, and parsley to the bowl. Add salt and pepper to taste and garnish with capers if desired. Toss to coat and serve immediately.

Sicilian Celery, Asian Pear, Fennel, and Orange Slaw with Toasted Hazelnuts

Yield: 4 servings

I adore this combination of sweet, tart, vegetal, and anise. Add it to your favorite grilled veggies or serve as a wonderful side dish to a light summer meal.

INGREDIENTS

2 tablespoons (30 ml) freshly squeezed orange juice
1 tablespoon (20 g) raw local honey
1 tablespoon (15 ml) red wine vinegar
½ teaspoon sea salt
½ teaspoon freshly ground black pepper
¼ cup (60 ml) extra virgin olive oil
1 fennel bulb, cored and thinly sliced
1 bunch organic celery, thinly sliced on the diagonal
1 Asian pear, cored and julienned on a mandoline
2 navel oranges, peeled and segmented
⅓ cup (50 g) toasted hazelnuts, chopped

METHOD OF PREPARATION:

1. In a large bowl, whisk together the orange juice, honey, red wine vinegar, salt, pepper, and olive oil.
2. Add the fennel, celery, pear, and oranges and toss to gently coat.
3. Top with the chopped hazelnuts and serve immediately.

Simply Divine Celery Broth

Yield: 4 servings

This simple celery broth is excellent for curing what ails you. Hydrating, balancing, and perfectly salty, it will make you feel better instantly.

INGREDIENTS

2 tablespoons (30 ml) olive oil
1 sweet onion, diced
6 garlic cloves, chopped
2 bunches organic celery, washed and chopped
2 cups (400 g) reserved celery juice pulp
4 cups (960 ml) vegetable stock
2 cups (480 ml) water
1 bay leaf
1 teaspoon sea salt
½ teaspoon freshly ground black pepper

METHOD OF PREPARATION:

1. Heat a large heavy-bottomed stockpot over medium heat. Add the olive oil and onion and sauté for 5 minutes or until the onion begins to wilt and soften.
2. Add the garlic and stir for 30 seconds or until fragrant.
3. Add the chopped celery and cook for 5 to 7 minutes or until the celery begins to soften.
4. Add the celery juice pulp, vegetable stock, water, bay leaf, salt, and pepper.

5. Increase the heat to high, bring the soup to a boil, and then reduce the heat and simmer for 30 minutes.
6. Strain the soup through a fine-mesh strainer, pushing through with the back of a wooden spoon to release all the celery flavor.
7. Add salt and pepper to taste for additional seasoning. Serve hot.

Baobab Gazpacho

Yield: 4 servings

Celery is salty and vegetal, baobab is sweet and tangy. They come together in this creamy gazpacho for a mouthful of flavor. Use tomatoes at the peak of their season for optimal flavor as well as vitamin content.

INGREDIENTS

3 organic celery stalks, chopped
1 organic English cucumber, chopped
6 large organic beefsteak tomatoes, chopped
¼ cup (10 g) organic basil leaves
¼ cup (60 ml) extra virgin olive oil
¼ cup (60 ml) aged sherry vinegar
2 tablespoons (20 g) baobab powder
1 teaspoon sea salt

METHOD OF PREPARATION:

1. Working in batches, puree the ingredients in a high-powered blender on high speed.
2. Transfer the smooth mixture to a large bowl or large mason jar and stir to mix all the flavors.
3. For best results, allow the soup to chill in the refrigerator for at least 2 hours, or even better overnight. Enjoy cold.

Spicy Purple Potato Salad

Yield: 6 servings

This is not your traditional potato salad; this one is crunchy, creamy, spicy, and oh so perfect paired with your favorite BBQ dishes. You will never go back to the traditional again.

INGREDIENTS

2 pounds (910 g) baby purple fingerling potatoes, halved
2 tablespoons (30 g) plus ½ teaspoon sea salt, divided
3 tablespoons (45 ml) avocado oil
½ teaspoon freshly ground black pepper
2 red serrano chiles, thinly sliced (seeded for less heat)
1 garlic clove, minced
½ cup (120 ml) apple cider vinegar
2 teaspoons light brown coconut sugar
2 organic celery stalks, thinly sliced on the diagonal
½ cup (20 g) celery leaves
½ cup (20 g) organic parsley leaves

METHOD OF PREPARATION:

1. Place the potatoes in a large pot of cold water and season with 2 tablespoons (30 g) of the salt. Bring to a boil over high heat, lower the heat to a simmer, and cook the potatoes until knife tender, 10 to 15 minutes. Drain and allow to cool.

2. Heat the avocado oil in a large nonstick skillet over medium heat. Add the drained potatoes and cook, stirring occasionally, until crispy, about 10 minutes. Season with the remaining ½ teaspoon salt and the pepper.
3. While the potatoes are cooking, make the dressing. In a small saucepan over medium heat, combine the chiles, garlic, vinegar, and brown sugar and bring to a gentle simmer. Cook until the sugar dissolves, about 2 minutes.
4. When the potatoes are crispy, add them to a large bowl. Toss them with the dressing and allow to cool slightly and soak up all the flavors.
5. When ready to serve, add the celery, celery leaves, and parsley to the potato mixture and toss to coat.

Celery Juice Pulp Fritters

Yield: 4 servings

These fritters are so easy, and this recipe uses the fibrous pulp you would traditionally throw away. Upcycle much?! You can make these with other pulp blends as well, so play around and get creative. I love to serve them with a tzatziki sauce made with almond or cashew yogurt.

INGREDIENTS

1 cup (200 g) reserved celery pulp
½ cup (20 g) organic parsley, roughly chopped
¼ cup (20 g) nutritional yeast or grated Parmesan cheese
1 large egg (see Note)
¼ cup (60 g) coconut oil

METHOD OF PREPARATION:

1. In a large bowl, combine the pulp, parsley, nutritional yeast or Parmesan, and egg.
2. Form the mixture into 4 large patties.
3. Heat the coconut oil in a large nonstick sauté pan over medium heat until hot.
4. Once the oil is hot, add the patties and fry for 2 to 3 minutes on one side or until golden brown.
5. Flip them gently and continue to cook on the other side for 2 to 3 minutes. Drain on a paper towel and serve hot.

Note: To make a vegan replacement for one egg, combine 3 tablespoons (45 ml) whipped aquafaba (the liquid from a can of chickpeas), ½ teaspoon sea salt, and ½ teaspoon freshly ground black pepper.

Green Juice Pulp Crackers

Yield: 4 servings

You will need a dehydrator for these crackers. You can use any blend of green juice pulp from the juice section. These are amazing with hummus or cashew cheese.

INGREDIENTS

1 cup (200 g) green juice pulp
¼ cup (28 g) organic ground flaxseed
¼ cup (44 g) organic chia seeds
¼ cup (20 g) nutritional yeast
2 tablespoons (16 g) sesame seeds
1 tablespoon (15 ml) tamari
1 teaspoon sea salt
⅛ teaspoon cayenne pepper
¼ cup (60 ml) water

METHOD OF PREPARATION:

1. In the bowl of a food processor, combine all the ingredients and process on high speed until thoroughly combined.
2. Line a dehydrator sheet pan with parchment paper. Spread the mixture on the prepared pan.
3. Score the crackers into the desired shape and size you wish to have.
4. Place the sheet pan in the dehydrator and cook for 5 hours at 115°F (46°C).
5. Flip the crackers over on the tray and continue to cook for 2 to 3 hours or until they are dried and crispy throughout.
6. Break the crackers apart on the score lines and store in an airtight container for up to 1 week.

Pulp-sicles

Yield: 6 servings

These can be made with any of the fruit-heavy juices and leftover pulp. You could even add a little prosecco to the mix and make a boozy pulp-sicle! You will also need an ice pop mold with sticks to make these.

INGREDIENTS

2 cups (400 g) leftover fruit pulp

½ cup (120 ml) fruit juice of your choice

METHOD OF PREPARATION:

1. Combine the pulp and juice in a high-speed blender and puree until smooth.
2. Pour into the ice pop molds and place the stick in the middle.
3. Freeze overnight and enjoy!

Celery Pulp Hummus

Yield: 12 servings

Here's another great upcycle trick! And a genius way to get some vegetables and fiber into your hummus. I love this made with celery and beet pulp, but play around and create your favorite. Serve with crudités or your favorite pita chips.

INGREDIENTS

One 16-ounce (455 g) can chickpeas, rinsed and drained
2 garlic cloves
1 teaspoon sea salt
1 tablespoon (8 g) ground cumin
1 tablespoon (8 g) ground coriander
½ cup (100 g) celery juice pulp or other veggie pulp
⅓ cup (80 g) tahini
¼ cup (60 ml) freshly squeezed lemon juice
6 tablespoons (90 ml) extra virgin olive oil, divided
¼ cup (60 ml) water
1 tablespoon (9 g) lightly toasted pine nuts
1 teaspoon paprika

METHOD OF PREPARATION:

1. In a food processor, add the chickpeas, garlic, salt, cumin, coriander, celery juice pulp, tahini, and lemon juice. Slowly add 4 tablespoons (60 ml) of the oil and the water. Scrape down the sides until the hummus is smooth. You may add more water if necessary, for your desired consistency.
2. Transfer the hummus to a serving bowl. Drizzle with the remaining 2 tablespoons (30 ml) olive oil and sprinkle with the toasted pine nuts and paprika.

Juice Pulp Veggie Burgers

Yield: 4 servings

I love these burgers made with the pulp from celery, kale, beet, and carrots, but play around and find your favorite combination.

INGREDIENTS

1 tablespoon (7 g) organic ground flaxseed
3 tablespoons (45 ml) water
2 cups (400 g) juice pulp
2 garlic cloves, minced
1 teaspoon sea salt
1 teaspoon freshly ground black pepper
1 teaspoon paprika
½ cup (120 g) canned black beans, drained and lightly mashed
2 tablespoons (30 ml) avocado oil

METHOD OF PREPARATION:

1. In a large bowl, combine the flaxseed and water and allow to sit for 15 minutes.
2. Add the juice pulp, garlic, salt, pepper, paprika, and beans and mix to combine.
3. Divide and shape into 4 burgers. Place in the refrigerator for 30 minutes.
4. Heat the oil in a large nonstick sauté pan over medium heat. Add the patties and cook for 4 to 5 minutes on one side, gently flip, and cook for 4 to 5 minutes on the other side.
5. Serve with your favorite toppings.

Juice Pulp "Meat" Balls

Yield: 4 servings

These "meat" balls are a tasty way to enjoy a meatless meal. I love them made with the pulp from kale, carrot, beet, and celery.

INGREDIENTS

2 cups (400 g) vegetable juice pulp
3 tablespoons (45 ml) aquafaba (liquid from a can of chickpeas) or 1 large egg
½ cup (50 g) nutritional yeast or grated Parmesan cheese
2 garlic cloves, minced
2 teaspoons dried basil
1½ teaspoons dried oregano
1 teaspoon sea salt

METHOD OF PREPARATION:

1. Preheat the oven to 375°F (190°C, or gas mark 5). Line a baking sheet with parchment paper and set aside.
2. In a large bowl, combine the pulp, aquafaba or egg, nutritional yeast or Parmesan, garlic, dried herbs, and salt. Mix to combine. With wet hands, form into 1-inch (2.5 cm) balls.
3. Place them on the prepared baking sheet 2 inches (5 cm) apart.
4. Transfer to the oven and bake for 15 minutes or until set and lightly browned.
5. Flip them over and bake for 15 minutes or until firm.
6. Serve with your favorite marinara sauce and low-carb pasta.

Juice Pulp Granola

Yield: 8 servings

This gluten-free, no-sugar-added granola is a great way to use up your leftover juicing pulp! Try different combinations for a fun spin on your morning granola. I love making this granola with a fruit-heavy juice pulp. You will need a dehydrator for this recipe.

INGREDIENTS

20 pitted Medjool dates
½ cup (40 g) unsweetened coconut flakes
3 cups (720 ml) juice pulp
2 cups (160 g) old-fashioned rolled oats
1 cup (150 g) goji berries

METHOD OF PREPARATION:

1. In the bowl of a food processor, add the dates, coconut flakes, and juice pulp. Process on high speed until the mixture is smooth.
2. Add the oats and goji berries and pulse until roughly chopped.
3. Place on a parchment-lined dehydrator pan in a thin layer and bake at 115°F (46°C) for 8 to 10 hours or until dry and crumbly.
4. Store in an airtight container for up to 1 week.

Pistachio Green Juice Pulp Pesto

Yield: About 3 cups (720 g)

This is an incredible way to get extra greens into your favorite pasta sauce. In this recipe, use the pulp of a juice made with kale, celery, parsley, chard, spinach, lettuce . . . you get the idea.

INGREDIENTS

½ cup (75 g) pistachio meat
2 garlic cloves
½ cup (50 g) nutritional yeast
3 cups (600 g) green juice pulp
1 cup (40 g) organic basil leaves
1 teaspoon sea salt
½ teaspoon freshly ground black pepper
¼ cup (60 ml) extra virgin olive oil
¼ cup (60 ml) water

METHOD OF PREPARATION:

1. In the bowl of a food processor, add the pistachio meat, garlic, and nutritional yeast. Process on high speed until finely minced.
2. Add the pulp, basil, salt, and pepper and process on high speed until everything is broken down.
3. With the motor running, add the olive oil and water and process until well combined.
4. Store in the refrigerator in an airtight container for up to 1 month.

Veggie-Packed Vegetable Broth

Yield: About 6 cups (1440 ml)

Use a vegetable-heavy juice pulp to make this delightful veggie broth. I love to have this on hand for soups and stews or even just to sip with spices when I'm feeling a little lethargic. I love to use a juice pulp packed with carrots, celery, kale, spinach, lettuce, chard, and parsley.

INGREDIENTS

8 cups (1920 ml) water
6 cups (1200 g) vegetable juice pulp
6 garlic cloves, smashed
1 tablespoon (15 g) sea salt
1 tablespoon (5 g) peppercorns
4 bay leaves

METHOD OF PREPARATION:

1. Combine all the ingredients in a large stockpot. Bring to a boil over high heat. Reduce the heat to low and let the broth simmer, uncovered, for 3 hours or until fragrant and flavorful.
2. Strain through a fine-mesh strainer and allow to cool before refrigerating.

Quarto

This edition published in 2024 by Chartwell Books, an imprint of The Quarto Group
142 West 36th Street, 4th Floor
New York, NY 10018 USA
T (212) 779-4972 F (212) 779-6058
www.Quarto.com

Contains content originally published as *The Celery Juice Book* in 2019 by Chartwell Books, an imprint of The Quarto Group, 142 West 36th Street, 4th Floor, New York, NY 10018 USA.

10 9 8 7 6 5 4 3 2 1

ISBN: 978-0-7858-4509-6

Publisher: Wendy Friedman
Creative Director: Laura Drew
Managing Editor: Cara Donaldson
Editor: Leeann Moreau
Cover Design: Alana Ward
Interior Design: Laura Drew

Printed in China

This book provides general information. It should not be relied upon as recommending or promoting any specific diagnosis or method of treatment for a particular condition, and it is not intended as a substitute for medical advice or for direct diagnosis and treatment of a medical condition by a qualified physician. Readers who have questions about a particular condition, possible treatments for that condition, or possible reactions from the condition or its treatment should consult a physician or other qualified medical professional.